Pumpkin Plant Parts

Matt Reher
Kristina Rupp

This is a pumpkin.

This is a pumpkin plant.

Pumpkin plants have leaves.

They have lots of leaves.

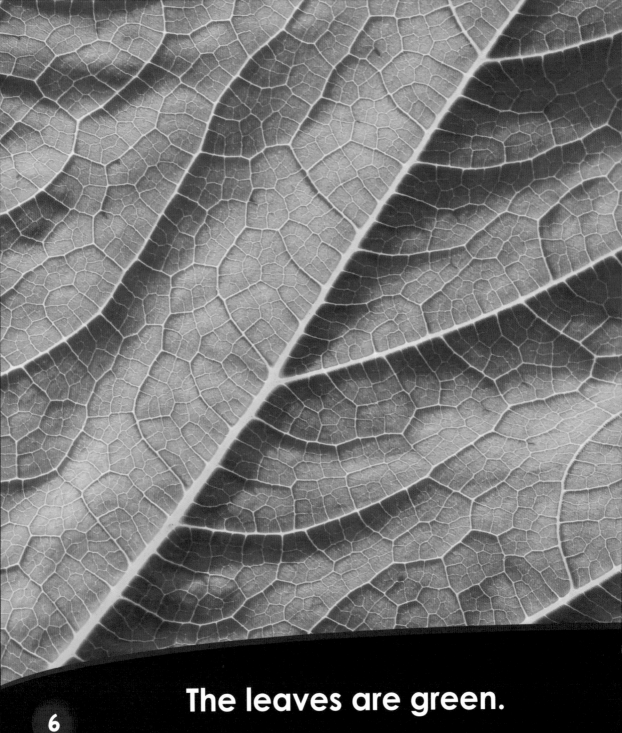

The leaves are green.

The leaves get sun.

food

The leaves make food.

The leaves make food
for the pumpkin plant.

Pumpkin plants have roots.

Roots get water.

Water goes up the roots.

The water goes from the
plant to the pumpkin.

This is how the pumpkin gets water.

This is a shell.

Shell

This is a pumpkin shell.

See the bugs.
Bugs love to eat pumpkins.

Bugs want to get into
the pumpkin to eat it.

The pumpkin shell stops the bugs. The bugs can't get in to eat the pumpkin.

Pumpkin
Plant Parts
The Vine

flower

tendrils

leaf

The Pumpkin

Pumpkins are a fruit. They are grown for their tasty seeds and meaty shell. Large pumpkins can weigh 9–18 pounds, but the biggest one ever grown weighed over 2000 pounds!

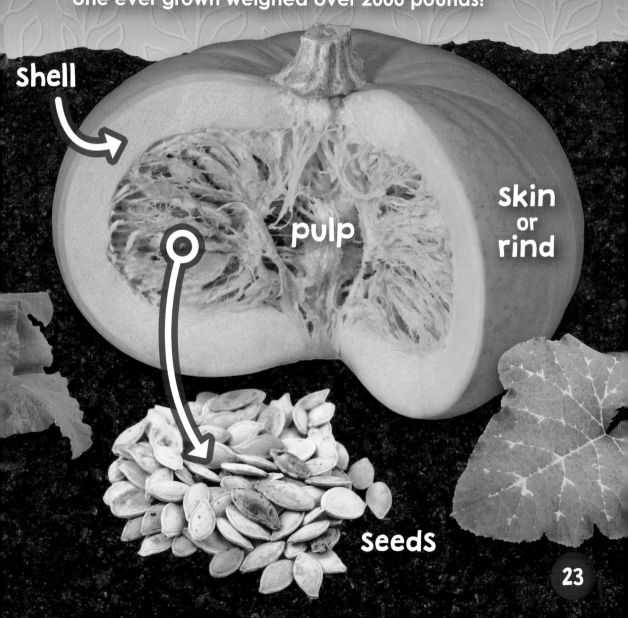

Shell

pulp

Skin or rind

seeds

Power Words

How many can you read?

a	have	see
are	how	stop
can't	in	the
eat	into	they
for	is	this
from	it	to
get	lots	up
goes	make	want
green	of	